Fred.Olsen Cruise Lines

John Hendy

The **Braemar** (Bruce Peter)

2

Contents

Produced and designed by Ferry Publications trading as Lily Publications Ltd

PO Box 33, Ramsey, Isle of Man, British Isles, IM99 4LP

Tel: +44 (0) 1624 898446   Fax: +44 (0) 1624 898449

www.ferrypubs.co.uk   E-Mail: info@lilypublications.co.uk

Printed and bound by Gomer Press Ltd., Wales, UK +44 (0) 1559 362371 © Lily Publications 2012

First Published: March 2012

Introduction

This is a book specifically concerning the ships of Fred. Olsen Cruise Lines, but which also outlines the origins, success and developments of the Company's passenger shipping business throughout the years.

Unlike many of the larger organisations that participate in the cruise market, the Fred. Olsen-related cruise activities build on more than 160 years' of proud maritime heritage, whilst maintaining a strong presence of the family interests that started it all. Fred. Olsen, the fourth generation, is the Chairman of the Boards of the two Oslo Stock Exchange-listed companies Bonheur ASA and Ganger Rolf ASA, which ultimately hold the shareholding interests in the cruise business. Fred. Olsen & Co, the sole proprietor of which is Fred. Olsen's daughter Anette Olsen, is in charge of the day-to-day management of these companies. Fred. Olsen's son, Fred. Junior, holds the position of Chairman of the Board of Fred. Olsen Cruise Lines Ltd.

Today, Fred. Olsen Cruise Lines is part of a group of companies with such diverse interests as oil tankers, alternative energy sources, land management and drilling operations.

In preparation for this book, the writer visited all four of the present Fred. Olsen Cruise Lines' fleet in the belief that if you are going to write about something, then you must first experience it for yourself. Having been individually sourced to fit the Company's specific requirements, every ship in the fleet is different in character, although certain common qualities shine through.

The ships are – without exception – most beautifully maintained and presented. There is a rolling programme of refurbishment and upgrade – exterior paintwork sparkles and is without rust, while the teak rails shine and decks are spotless. Cleaning the ships' interiors is also a continuous fixture and all credit must go to the hard-working crews for both attaining and maintaining these consistently high standards.

As the vessels fall into the medium-sized category of cruise ships, guests find their layout both easy to navigate and to get to know. As the large majority of public rooms are situated on a single deck

*The **Balmoral** is seen in the Kiel Canal. (Marko Stampehl)*

or clustered towards the ships' after ends, it really is difficult to lose oneself on board. A further advantage of operating a fleet of smaller-sized cruise ships is that they are often able to access ports which the large and impersonal 'Noah's Arks' of the cruise industry are frequently unable to reach. Fred. Olsen ships have been traditionally designed and inevitably appear just as the clientele expect their ships to look.

Whenever on board a Fred. Olsen ship, the Company interest in its nautical heritage is readily evident. Maritime tradition and traditional values play a large and important part in the overall on board experience, which the British find so hard to resist. This ranges from large ship models of the Fred. Olsen fleet – past and present – to fine oil paintings and impressive bronze figureheads from previous ships. Fred. Olsen has rejected the glitz, bright lights, loud music and razzamataz of other operators and has established a niche market within the UK cruise industry. As the publicity material states, 'more country house than Las Vegas' and with the majority of its customers being both British and retired, ship interiors are suitably peaceful, quiet in colour palette and restful on the eye. Even examples of modern art, which members of the Olsen family choose carefully themselves, are not so garish as to distract and overwhelm guests. Music is restrained, afternoon tea may be taken while listening to the tinkle of a grand piano and each ship offers the opportunity to escape and relax far away from the relentless pace and rigour of everyday life.

And finally, there are the hard-working crews who are always happy to greet guests with a ready smile and are genuinely pleased to see you. This, added to the comfortable and welcoming fleet of ships, is a key part of the Company's success and is the product of the family-run business that is Fred. Olsen Cruise Lines.

John Hendy
Ivychurch, Romney Marsh, Kent
March 2012

Chapter 1

FRED. OLSEN AND SHIPPING - AN OVERVIEW

With a population of almost five million, more than three-quarters of the Norwegian people live within ten miles of the sea. With so much of the country offering an inhospitable environment in which to farm, Norwegians have traditionally turned to the sea for their living. Norway became independent from Sweden in 1905 when the new kingdom's requirement for overseas trade was vital for its future prosperity and well-being. Initially, this was with Norway's close North Sea neighbours, but soon spread to become worldwide.

Life was frequently difficult during the early years of independence and large numbers of Norwegians emigrated to the United States. As it was not until 1913 that a trans-Atlantic service was established, the vast majority of those wishing to seek a fresh start in the New World crossed the North Sea to Britain before setting out to cross the ocean, and hence a new trade was established.

THE OLSENS OF HVITSTEN

The Olsen family lived at Hvitsten, a tiny settlement situated on the east side of Oslofjord, in the narrows before the great fjord widens out between Horten and Moss.

The first Olsen family ship owner was Fredrik Christian Olsen, who started the business in 1848 and initially operated a fleet of well-tried sailing vessels. Trade quickly flourished and larger ships even traded to the United States. His brothers, Petter and Andreas, were also involved in coastal trading and Petter's son Thomas Fredrik (the second Fred. Olsen) was a successful sea Captain who eventually took charge of his father's fleet. The largest of his ships was the Canadian-built full-rigger *Morning Light,* which is today commemorated by the presence of the 'Morning Light Pub' on both the *Balmoral* and *Braemar*. By the time that Fredrik Christian died in 1875, he had owned 22 ships.

Fred. Olsen ordered his first steam ship in 1896 from a local shipyard in Christiania (later Oslo). This was the third company vessel named *Bayard* and was deployed on the Northern France service to Garston, on the Lancashire bank of the River Mersey upriver from Liverpool. Since that launch, it has become the tradition that most Fred. Olsen ships have a name beginning with 'B'. Following Petter's death in 1899, Fred. moved the Company headquarters from Hvitsten to Christiania and fast expansion followed, particularly on the Baltic and North Sea services, as he purchased a number of smaller companies, their ships and

The first generation: (left to right) Fredrik Christian Olsen, Andreas Olsen, Petter Olsen (Fred. Olsen archives)

established routes. Amongst these was a cargo link with Rouen in 1900 and a passenger and cargo link with Grangemouth (near Edinburgh), which Olsen started in 1901. Further ties with Antwerp and Newcastle commenced in 1906, with Rotterdam following in 1912.

PASSENGER TRADE

The start of the passenger ship trade to Grangemouth in 1901 is of importance in the Company's development. Three ships, named *Faerder*, *Scotland* and *Norway*, were acquired. Each carried 100 passengers, the latter two being fitted with electric lighting, thus making them extremely modern vessels at that time. It was perhaps as well that Olsen held a considerable share in the Aker shipyard in Christiania, as five years later a further fleet acquisition opened the door to Newcastle and two new ships, the *Sterling* and *Sovereign,* were immediately ordered. The Antwerp service also saw new tonnage in the *Brussel* and *Brabant*, followed in 1910 by the 80-passenger *Paris*.

By the outbreak of World War I in 1914, the Olsen fleet numbered 40 ships and, after the opening of the Panama Canal in

*The **Scotland** of 1889 was built at Grangemouth and was purchased by Fred. Olsen for the Oslo service in 1903. She could carry 100 passengers and was lit by electricity. (Fred. Olsen archives)*

the following year, services to South America and the west coast of the USA and Canada were operated. Although throughout the war, Norway remained firmly neutral, and all ships were marked with the word 'Norge' along their hulls, this sadly failed to prevent losses due to magnetic mines and 'U' boats. With the majority of Norway's merchant ships sailing for the Allies, half the Olsen fleet was lost.

An early ship powered by the revolutionary diesel engine was Olsen's *Brazil* of 1914 for the South American trade. Following the Armistice in 1918, the Company set about replacing its war losses with either new or suitably-sourced second-hand tonnage.

Further expansion occurred in 1921 when a contract was gained to import fruit from Spain and the Canary Islands to London's West India Docks, which was named after the islands – the instantly recognisable 'Canary Wharf' - at which the Company later built a new terminal. In order to operate this important trade successfully, a special requirement was speed, so that the perishable fruit could be delivered while it was still fresh. With this in mind, during the 1930s a new series of vessels was built specifically to carry the fruit, and hulls were painted pale grey rather than black, in order to reflect more sunlight and so lower the

temperature in the ships' holds. The later ships in the series started carrying figureheads, thus reviving memories of the sailing ship era, some of which are placed on board the four Fred. Olsen cruise ships today.

Fred. Olsen & Company – a partnership between Fred. Olsen with his sons Rudolf and Thomas and a Mr JLM Miller – had been established in 1915. When the second Fred. Olsen died in 1933, the fleet was 60 strong and that same year also saw Rudolf and Thomas Olsen take the Company into the airline trade. This business eventually developed into Scandinavian Airlines System (SAS), although Company interests in this and other majority- owned airlines has since ceased.

The brief interval of European peace had seen great strides in the development of the marine diesel engine, which Olsen marked by the introduction of the third-named *Brabant* in 1926. As its first motor-driven passenger vessel, the 2,335-gross-ton ship could carry 100 passengers, with as many as 70 in First Class accommodation. For the Antwerp service, there followed the third-named *Bretagne* in 1938, which introduced a new yellow funnel emblazoned with the Company house flag.

*The **Sovereign**, built in Middlesbrough in 1886, was taken over by Fred. Olsen in 1906 and was used on the Newcastle service. (Fred. Olsen archives)*

*The second named **Sterling** was purpose-built for the Newcastle route and was placed in service during 1907. She was the first of the Company's passenger vessels to be built in Norway. (Fred. Olsen archives)*

BLACK PRINCE AND BLACK WATCH

During 1938 and immediately before the outbreak of war, competition on the North Sea trades had seen Olsen introduce the splendid 5,035-gross-ton *Black Prince* and *Black Watch,* which were named in honour of England and Scotland. These ships represented the last word in luxury and comfort and carried 185 First Class and 65 Second Class passengers. Crossing the North Sea at 18 knots, their passage to Oslo took 32 hours, although some chose to leave the ships at Kristiansand and travel to the capital by train, thereby saving nine hours. Sadly, neither vessel was to achieve her potential; seized by the Germans while laid up in a Norwegian fjord in April 1940, they both became accommodation ships before being lost in the turmoil of war. Happily, both their figureheads were recovered and later reused.

Of the Olsen brothers, Rudolf remained in Norway, but Thomas escaped with his family to the UK and then to the US. At the outbreak of war, the Company owned 57 ships, but was sadly to lose 28 vessels and 189 men in the forthcoming world conflict.

Used on the pre-war passenger service to Antwerp, it was the *Bretagne* which re-opened the service to Newcastle in August 1945. Although later joined by the elderly steamer *Bali*, replacements for the *Black Prince* and *Black Watch* were badly needed, but as the Aker yard in Oslo was then enjoying a full post-war order book, the hulls were constructed by Thorneycroft at Southampton and then towed to Oslo to be engined and fitted-out.

In honour of Sir Winston Churchill, the first of the new twins was named *Blenheim* after the stately home of his birth and entered service between Oslo and Newcastle in March 1951. Sister ship, *Braemar,* followed in May 1953.

The futuristic appearance of these remarkable-looking vessels was the result of wind tunnel tests and they displayed extremely streamlined superstructures with funnel and mast conjoined into one. The fully air-conditioned pair were both a shade under 4,800 gross tons, while accommodation for the premier ship was for 101 First Class, 100 Tourist Class and 36 Group Class passengers. As a sign of the changing times, some 40 cars could be stored in the holds and were craned on board at either end of the journey; however, this aspect of their design was all too soon to cause problems and in the years to come they frequently suffered from capacity constraints.

Shortly before the *Blenheim* entered service, Rudolf Olsen had died in February 1951. His loss was compounded four years later when Thomas Olsen suffered a debilitating stroke and was no longer able to continue running the business. At the age of just 26, his son – the third Fred. Olsen – now took control of the Company, where he is still the Chairman.

CAR FERRIES AND A JOINT SERVICE

With the sharp increase in passengers wishing to travel with their cars across the North Sea, Fred. Olsen's Norwegian rival the Bergen Steamship Company was also suffering from a lack of vehicle space on its own ferry service to Newcastle. Resulting from this, a fascinating and unusual joint agreement was reached, although the ownership of the first jointly-owned ship was 52 per cent in Olsen's favour. A new stern-loading vehicle ferry was ordered from Lübeck in Germany and was designed to lead a dual existence. During the summer months, she would operate as a conventional car ferry for the Bergen Line, carrying 587 passengers and 184 cars under the

*The **Brabant** of 1924 was Fred. Olsen's first motor-driven passenger ship and was principally engaged on the Oslo - Antwerp service. Her funnel and masts were added in 1937. (Fred. Olsen archives)*

*In 1938, Olsen introduced the magnificent sisters **Black Prince** and **Black Watch** which were both casualties of the Second World War. (Fred. Olsen Cruise Lines)*

name of *Jupiter*. At the end of the season, some 48 hours were all that was required to change the ship's identity to Olsen's *Black Watch*. The car decks were converted into refrigerated cargo spaces for the import of fruit and tomatoes, the smaller cabins were closed up, the cafeteria became a restaurant and seats were removed to reveal a hidden swimming pool. The conversion complete, the *Black Watch* was ready to transport 350 passengers on cruises to the Canaries (and later Madeira).

The sister ship *Black Prince* was initially owned outright by Olsen and operated an alternating summer service from Kristiansand to Amsterdam and Harwich. The passenger ship *Blenheim* was tragically gutted by fire in May 1968, after which she was laid aside, leaving the *Braemar* to continue the Oslo-

Kristiansand-Newcastle sailings alone until her eventual withdrawal in 1975.

The success of the twin car ferries saw a larger version built by Upper Clyde Shipbuilders. This was the 10,420-gross-ton *Blenheim*, which revived the name of the 1951-built ship. Built with the grant system then available from the British Government, the *Blenheim*'s time at the Clydebank yard proved to be a somewhat torrid period with strikes, thefts and extremely difficult industrial relations. Due to be delivered in February 1970, the ship missed the season and was seven months late, causing Fred. Olsen the inconvenience of chartering a vessel in her place. A similar-looking, but altogether larger ship than the twins, the *Blenheim* carried 995 passengers and 300 cars.

The very modern-looking and streamlined **Blenheim** *(1951) and* **Braemar** *(1953) were built at Southampton but were towed to Oslo for fitting out. They were engaged on the Oslo - Kristiansand - Newcastle link. (Fred. Olsen archives)*

KDS SKAGERAK EXPRESS

During 1968, Olsen had sold a part interest in the *Black Prince* to Bergen Line (on a 60/40 per cent basis) and, as from 1970, she operated as the *Venus* when engaged on her summer North Sea crossings. The year 1968 also saw Olsen purchase KDS (the Kristiansand Steamship Company), which operated the busy four-hour Skagerak Express service between Kristiansand and Hirtshals in Denmark for passengers, vehicles and railway wagons. This effectively switched the centre of the Olsen ferry business to the south of Norway and, during the next few years, a degree of interchange occurred between certain ships on this route, the traditional North Sea services and the Canary Islands fruit runs.

An early introduction was the motor vessel *Buenavista* for summer car traffic and winter Canaries fruit operation. She was followed by the *Bonanza* and then in 1973 by the 11,344 gross ton *Bolero*, a car ferry/cruise ship built at Nantes in France. She had been acquired second-hand after the Sweden-Germany service for which she was built, had failed to materialise, although Olsen owned a share in her. The vessel eventually sailed across the Atlantic, running summer seasons between Portland (Maine) and Yarmouth (Nova Scotia), but the winter months saw her sail to Miami for an entirely different trade. Operating for Commodore Cruise Line, the *Bolero* was used to run Caribbean cruises and thus it can be claimed that she was the first Fred. Olsen cruise ship. The Aalborg-built *Borgen* followed in 1975 and was principally used on

*The car ferry **Blenheim** was constructed on the Clyde in 1970 as a larger version to the sisters **Black Watch** and **Black Prince**. She was sold for cruising in the Caribbean during 1981. (FotoFlite)*

the Skagerak service, although she did occasionally run to Newcastle and Harwich.

During a period of intense competition on the North Sea routes, in October 1981 Fred. Olsen and Bergen Line chartered their *Venus* and *Jupiter* to the Danish company DFDS for a period of three years. DFDS also purchased the *Blenheim* and converted her into a cruise ship for the American market. The upshot of this agreement was that the popular Kristiansand-Harwich link was severed for the 1982 season, although Olsen restarted it in summer 1984, using the

Bolero on a once-a-week basis. The 1985 season saw DFDS continue the charter of the *Black Watch/Jupiter* for one more season, while the *Black Prince/Venus* was chartered to the newly formed Norway Line for its summer Newcastle-Bergen link.

Two purchases from Sally Line (part of the Viking Line consortium) occurred in 1984 and 1985. First, came the 5,288-gross-ton *Bolette*, followed a year later by the substantial, second-named *Braemar* (14,623 gross tons), a 2,000-passenger vessel which, following a refit at Hamburg, entered service on the

Skagerak Express link, which included a weekly crossing to Harwich. Her white hull was a first from Olsen and the rest of the fleet soon followed suit.

Olsen's next move was to purchase the redundant Sheerness-Vlissingen ferry *Olau Britannia* (14,982 gross tons), which had been replaced by a larger ferry of the same name in May 1990. As the *Bayard* (the eighth Olsen ship to be thus named), the ship entered service in the Skagerak during the following month. Also during June, the recently-refitted *Bolero* made her first visit to the Tyne, allowing the larger *Braemar* to be transferred to the Oslo-Hirtshals route, which had been experiencing capacity problems. The decision to operate from a single UK terminal had been taken in September 1989 when the Harwich service ceased.

This was almost the end for the Fred. Olsen ferry business in Northern Europe, as towards the close of 1990 the *Braemar* was sold to a Cypriot concern, after which she took up the Leningrad-Stockholm route as the *Anna Karenina*. Then, on 15th December 1990, it was announced that Fred. Olsen's North Sea and Skagerak passenger services, along with the *Bolero*, *Bayard* and *Borgen*, had been sold for £103.6 million to the newly-formed Color Line, although the purely freight services continued.

This move very much represented the end of an era and the closing of a long and respected tradition for the Olsen Company. Apart from its tanker and oil-rig work, the Company was now left with its car ferry services in the Canary Islands and Morocco, and also with the *Black Prince* now engaged in full-time cruising (see page 20).

A TRANSPORT REVOLUTION IN THE CANARIES

The Spanish Canary Islands form a 250-mile long archipelago consisting of seven large islands and a number of smaller islets. The group lies in the Atlantic Ocean off the coast of north west Africa and is volcanic in origin and nature. With the Canary Islands now a popular European holiday destination, the Fred. Olsen Express service has completely transformed inter-island services, and represents a huge financial input into the islands' economy.

Ships of the Fred. Olsen Company commenced trading with the islands during 1920, taking over the Otto Thoresen fleet, which had commenced service in 1904. The Olsen family had owned land on the isolated island of La Gomera since before the First World War. The production of tomatoes and bananas became increasingly important for the growing British market and regular calls were

*Top: The French-built vehicle ferry **Bolero** entered service in 1973 and joined the Fred. Olsen fleet in 1982. (Bruce Peter collection)*

*Above: The **Bolette** dated from 1974 and was completed as the **Viking 5** before joining the KDS Skagerak Express fleet in 1984. Four years later she passed to Comarit and was renamed **Boughaz** (see page 18). (Bruce Peter collection)*

Top: The 96-metre **Bentago Express** *dates from 2000 and was the third of Fred. Olsen's 'Express' vessels. She accommodates 941 passengers and 270 cars. (InCat)*

Above: The **Barlavento** *was the final traditional vehicle ferry in service before fast ferries took over the complete route system in 2005. (Matt Davies)*

made to ship them to the aptly named Canary Wharf in London. However, it was the introduction of the *Black Watch* and the *Black Prince* in the mid 1960s that was perhaps the catalyst for the Company's present-day involvement in the region.

During 1974, Ferry Gomera SA was founded to operate a 20-mile service from the island to the adjacent island of Tenerife. A small 887-gross-ton car ferry named *Benchijigua* was delivered from Norwegian builders, able to carry 400 passengers and 60 cars.

With some 25,000 passengers already transported during that first half year of operation, success was assured and by 1980 the ship was proving to be far too small. Accordingly, the 1972-built *Bonanza* (750 passengers/200 cars) was transferred from the Skagerak route to take her place and name. At this time, the first ship was switched to open the eastern route between the islands of Fuerteventura and Lanzarote, for which she was renamed *Betancuria*.

Unfortunate technical problems saw the service suspended and the ship eventually sold to Icelandic owners. After further delays, it was not until July 1989 that a small, second-hand Norwegian-built ship was put on the route. Built as the fjord ferry *Tungenes* in 1966, she had latterly been working in the German Baltic before being renamed *Betancuria* and was eventually sold out of service in 1996.

A further ship joined the fleet in 1992 in the form of the *Buganvilla*, a German-built car ferry constructed for the short service across the Oresund linking Sweden and Denmark. Originally the *Betula*, the compact little vessel accommodated 1,000 passengers and 105 cars on the Fuerteventura-Lanzarote service.

It should perhaps be mentioned at this point in the narrative that, in the Canaries, it has been the Company practice to link specific ship names with the routes on which they operate. For a vessel that was later transferred to another route, a change of name was inevitably required.

With the Company's North Sea and Skagerak passenger services having been disposed of in 1990, three years later Ferry Gomera reinvented itself as 'Lineas Fred. Olsen'. The time was now right for further expansion and to take on the established operators throughout the archipelago. In 1994, a larger *Benchijigua* was placed on service in the islands when the previous ship of that name became the *Bajamar*. The new ship boasted an interesting pedigree, having been built at Bremerhaven as the *Djursland II* in 1974 for Danish internal work. With accommodation for 1,500 passengers and 370 cars, she was the largest ferry yet and was later placed on the new Gran Canaria-Lanzarote service. Also that year, the Company acquired P&O Ferries' *Pride of Cherbourg*; the Aalborg-built ship boasted a capacity for 1,286 passengers and 275 cars and was formerly Townsend Thoresen's *Viking Voyager*. Originally named *Banaderos* for the central islands link between Tenerife and Gran Canaria, five years later she was renamed *Barlavento* when she was switched to work between Tenerife and the western islands of La Palma and El Hierro, the smallest of the main islands in the archipelago. The final link is now the *Benchijigua* sailing between Lanzarote / Fuerteventura and Gran Canaria – completing services for all of the islands.

FRED. OLSEN EXPRESS

By now, Lineas Fred. Olsen had established itself as the largest operator in the Canary Islands group and looked to substantially cut inter-island timings by introducing high-speed craft. The first was a small surface effect ship capable of carrying up to 300 passengers at speeds of 40 knots. Originally named *Sant Agata*, she later briefly ran as the *Wight King* from Southampton to Cowes on the Isle of Wight until purchased by Lineas Fred. Olsen in 1994 and named *Bahia Express* for an unprecedented 35-minute service linking the islands of Tenerife and La Gomera. Although the experiment gave the Company valuable experience with operating fast craft, she proved to be too small and was sold on three years later.

A new company, Canaria de Buques Rapidos SA, now ordered a trio of 96-metre catamarans from InCat of Hobart, Tasmania. The *Bonanza Express* was followed by the *Bentayga Express* (later renamed *Bencomo Express* in 1999). Capable of carrying 750/1,000 passengers and 230/300 cars respectively at speeds of over 40 knots, they effectively sliced crossing times between the islands in half. Although the second craft was originally intended to operate on the Tenerife-La Gomera route, with the appropriate name of *Benchijigua Express*, her new shore installations were incomplete and so she joined her sister vessel, with a quick change of name, on the 60-minute service linking the principal islands of Tenerife and Gran Canaria. The *Bonanza Express* presently operates a daily two-hour service from Tenerife to the south western island of El Hierro in addition to sailings to La Gomera.

The third of the InCat trio appeared in 2000 and, with the shore installations now ready, the 941-passenger/270-car vessel was named *Benchijigua Express* for the La Gomera route. She remained there until replaced by the new trimaran in 2005 at which time she was renamed *Bentago Express*. Today, she also operates on the Tenerife-Gran Canaria route.

By the advent of the new millennium, the Fred. Olsen Express craft had completely revolutionised transport between the islands. A fourth catamaran, the smaller *Bocayna Express*, arrived from Austal Ships of Fremantle in 2003 and with her capacity of 450 passengers and 69 cars, was placed on the 20-minute crossing linking the eastern islands of Fuerteventura and Lanzarote.

The fifth high-speed craft to be introduced was the spectacular Austal Ships trimaran *Benchijigua Express*. With a capacity of 1,291 passengers and 341 cars and with speeds in excess of 40 knots, she is claimed to be the world's largest multi-hulled ship. Today she operates with the *Bonanza Express* on the Tenerife-La Gomera crossing with additional services to the western island of La Palma which she completes in two hours.

A small 330-passenger-only 40-metre catamaran was added to the fleet in March 2009. The *Benchi Express* was leased from the Italian company SNAV to operate three times a day between Tenerife and three ports on La Gomera. Apart from the principal town of San Sebastian, the smaller ports of Valle Gran Rey and Playa Santiago are also visited as the larger vessels are unable to dock there.

The final link in the chain was added during summer 2011 when the Company chartered the spare Swedish car ferry *Thjelvar* for use on the Gran Canaria - Fuerteventura - Lanzarote service. The ship is the first conventional vessel to be employed since the *Barlovento* was sold in 2005. Renamed *Betancuria*, the new ferry links the central and eastern islands of the Canaries group.

Fred. Olsen's success in the Canary Islands has been remarkable. The seven islands are presently served by eight different routes and some 2.7 million passengers, 550,000 cars and over 200,000 lorries are carried each year.

The introduction of the Fred. Olsen Express fleet inevitably saw the withdrawal from service and departure of the conventional vessels, the *Barlavento* being the last to leave in 2005. The advent of fast sea passages has been welcomed by both islanders and holidaymakers who view the Olsen services as an extension of the existing road network.

Without doubt, Fred. Olsen Express has brought the islands and their people closer together than at any time in their history.

*Top: The **Bismillah** was Fred. Olsen's first vessel employed on a seasonal basis across the Strait of Gibraltar and operated between 1984 and 2006. (Miles Cowsill)*

*Above: The **Boughaz** was another former Skagerak Express ferry which joined the new Tangier - Algeciras service in 1988. (John May)*

AND SO TO AFRICA

The Kingdom of Morocco was no stranger to the ships of Fred. Olsen and Co., which had first called there in 1929. Trade increased in the period up to the 1960s but the shipment of citrus fruits by non-Moroccan tonnage was to be made increasingly difficult by the Moroccan Government. Matters came to a head in August 1979 when they decreed that all cargoes to and from Moroccan ports were to be reserved for Moroccan ships.

Olsen's response to this came in August 1981 when, together with local interests, the five Olsen-owned shipping companies formed Comarit (Compagnie Maritime Maroco-Norvegienne). The new company would transport citrus fruit but as this was mainly winter trade, any ships used in this work would require alternative employment during the summer months.

Traffic across the narrow Straits of Gibraltar from Spain to Morocco was blossoming as hundreds of thousands of migrant workers returned home to visit friends and families for long summer breaks. They did not require either fast or particularly luxurious tonnage in which to travel but reliable, well-tried ships which could maintain a steady schedule. Ever the experts at sourcing suitable tonnage for new enterprises, Olsen believed that it knew the right ship with which to commence its service.

Comarit firstly introduced the *Buenavista* which had been built in 1971 for the Skagerak Express service. Although she had left the route for a Baltic charter in 1982, her services were acquired in April 1984 and in the Olsen naming tradition of using the letter 'B', she was appropriately renamed *Bismillah* which was not only an historic company name but also served as a Muslim blessing. The ship was used for cargo runs to northern Europe during the winter months but in the first summer, problems with the existing ferry companies and the Spanish authorities meant that she had to be employed on the less-desirable Tangier-Malaga route from June 1984. Although Comarit now had a foot in the door, considerable obstacles had to be overcome before the company was allowed to operate its ship on the preferred two-hour link to Algeciras. Both Moroccan and Spanish authorities shared a pooling agreement with each taking 50 per cent of the passenger traffic and there was initial reluctance to allow a new operator to upset the *status quo*. Eventually, it was decided that Comarit could take 16 per cent of the overall traffic (about one third of the Moroccan share) and the first sailing between Tangier and Algeciras took place on 23rd July 1984. Within two years, the new company was already into profit.

Such was the success of the new Comarit service that in 1988, another former Skagerak Express ferry joined the link. This was the 1974-built *Bolette* which was renamed *Boughaz* for her new service. Built as one of a series of successful ferries at Papenburg in West Germany, she was originally Viking Line's *Viking 5*. In 1981 she was renamed *The Viking* for Sally Line's new Ramsgate-Dunkirk West route before eventually proving too small, passing to Olsen and becoming its sixth-named *Bolette* in 1984. The ship accommodates 1,200 passengers and 220 cars, and her entry into service allowed a year-round link to be offered.

Until 1992, the *Bismillah* operated as a ferry during the summer and a fruit carrier during the winter months but age was catching up with her and the 20-year-old ship was becoming less suitable for winter work. It was therefore decided that she should be used on the year-round ferry service and in this role she continued until 2003.

A third ferry was added in 1996 in the form of the *Banasa*. She was originally the *Mette Mols*, which had been built for internal Danish work during 1975. At 11,668 gross tons she boasted capacity for as many as 1,600 passengers and 420 cars thereby greatly boosting the route's patronage and income.

In the following year it was now deemed to be politically expedient to form a Spanish subsidiary company and accordingly, 'Lineas Maritimas Europeas' was registered and the *Boughaz* was transferred into their ownership. This made no difference to the published timetable or to the way in which the growing fleet was worked but served to strengthen the Company's position in Spain in addition to giving them an extra slot within the existing pooling arrangement.

The time was now right for further expansion in the east of Morocco and the longer Nador-Almeria route was added in 1999 as was the later 36-hour link between Nador and the French port of Sete. The tonnage eventually sourced to run these extra services consisted of two redundant SNCM Corsican ferries, the first of which was the large and very fast 20,079 gross ton *Napoleon* which had been built in 1976 and carried in excess of 2,000 passengers and 435 cars. The 24-knot ship was renamed *Berkane* and was joined in the fleet during 2003 by the *Liberte* which was renamed *Biladi*. At 18,913 gross tons, she boasted accommodation for 1,812 passengers and 500 cars. That same year saw the charter of the former Fred. Olsen vessel *Betancuria* which had been sold to Egyptian owners in the previous year and renamed *Sara 1*. She was initially used on a further new route

*Top: The **Black Prince** in her ferry role and seen against a Canary Islands backdrop. (Bruce Peter collection)*

*Above: Fred. Olsen's first cruise ship, the **Black Prince**. (Fred. Olsen Cruise Lines)*

from Al Hoceima to Almeria, but after the 35-year-old *Bismillah* was withdrawn, she was duly switched to the Tangier-Algeciras route at which time the seasonal Al Hoceima crossing was left in the hands of chartered tonnage. The *Sara 1* was eventually sold for scrapping in April 2010.

During the period 2002 to 2007, competition across the Strait of Gibraltar had grown to new levels with no fewer than eight companies competing for the traffic. The old sharing agreement was abandoned in 2004 by which time Comarit carried some 20 per cent of all traffic across the Straits. The same year saw the ending of the citrus trade with the Company focusing on its ferry links while in 2006 Olsen increased its share holding in Comarit to 55 per cent.

The privatisation of the state-operated and rival Moroccan ferry company Comanav in 2007 saw its purchase by the French group CMA CGM which passed the operational control to Comarit in 2009 thereby integrating the workings of both concerns. The *Berkane* was almost immediately switched to the former Comanav route from Tangier to Genoa.

With a fleet of five conventional ferries, with an average age of almost 30 years, the Comarit business had certainly brought Fred. Olsen shareholders some healthy dividends during the 25-year period of their operation. However, during June 2008, Olsen sold its 55 per cent share in Comarit to its Moroccan partners at which time its interest and input into these trades effectively ceased.

FRED. OLSEN CRUISE LINES

Fred. Olsen Cruise Lines presently operates four quite distinctive vessels. Although each is defined by her own individual fittings and personality, the ships are undeniably extensions of each other, and embody that unique ambience for which the Company is so well known and admired.

The ship that started it all was the much-loved *Black Prince* which, after an exemplary career was finally withdrawn from service in 2009. During the early days of cruising, the Company's experience, which stemmed from the *Black Prince*'s long and successful period of operation, enabled it to grow its market and thus to develop and flourish on a far greater scale. Looking to expand, Fred. Olsen carefully selected well-built ships, which have since been extensively modified and updated to suit the unique Fred. Olsen style.

BLACK PRINCE

During late 1965, Fred. Olsen & Co. ordered a new 9,500-gross-ton passenger and cargo liner which was duly launched at the German yard of Lübecker Flender-Werke on 4th May 1966 by the wife of the Lord Mayor of London – Lady Doris Denny. The vessel was named *Black Prince*.

As has been seen, rather oddly, the new ship was to enjoy a dual role, operating as a one-class passenger ship and fruit carrier between London and the Canary Islands between October and May (winter season), before inaugurating a new 22-hour two-class summer car ferry service between Harwich and Kristiansand in May 1967.

The new 13-day London-Canary Islands round service was jointly operated with a sister vessel, the *Black Watch*, which during the summer became Bergen Line's *Jupiter*. In 1970, after Bergen Line had purchased a share in her. The *Black Prince* also adopted the seasonal Bergen Line alias of *Venus*.

Yard number 561 was delivered in October 1966, although her sister ship had already operated throughout the summer as the *Jupiter*. During their first winter of 1966/67, both sisters operated as passenger liners on the Olsen service from London (Millwall Docks) to the Canary Islands of Gran Canaria and Tenerife, also calling at Madeira in later years in order to pick up large quantities of fruit for the UK market which was carried in their refrigerated lower car deck space. In this role the ships carried some 350 cruise passengers. Her first winter service completed, on 19th May 1967, the *Black Prince* duly took up the Harwich-Kristiansand route on which she carried 591 passengers and 185 cars.

For the 1970 season, Fred. Olsen took delivery of the slightly larger *Blenheim*, with which Olsen made a similar joint ownership arrangement with the Bergen Steamship Company (BDS). Following the introduction of the new ship, the *Black Prince* shared the Newcastle-Bergen route each summer, sailing as the *Venus*, while also working some Bergen-Amsterdam sailings. Her winter schedules were also to change when some Rotterdam-Canaries cruises were introduced when she was replaced on the London-Canaries cycle by the new *Blenheim*. As the Rotterdam services did not carry fruit, a more leisurely fortnightly schedule was provided, with calls at Lisbon, Casablanca, Madeira, Las Palmas and Tenerife.

This rather unusual arrangement continued with the sister ships maintaining split personalities, the only livery change being visible on their funnels which alternated between the Fred. Olsen and

*The **Black Prince** arriving at St Petersburg in June 2009. (Bob Blowers)*

Bergen Line house flags. The arrangement continued until 1975 after which the summer services were operated under the joint title of Fred. Olsen - Bergen Line. The funnels then retained the Fred. Olsen house flag throughout the year but were also adorned by the three white bands of the Bergen Line.

Danish operators DFDS now became involved during a period of expansion on the North Sea and for the summers of 1982-84 they chartered the *Venus* and the *Jupiter* on Bergen-Newcastle and Bergen-Amsterdam routes. This arrangement ended in 1984 and in the following year the Bergen-Newcastle service was taken over by the Bergen-based Norway Line who sub-chartered the *Venus/Black Prince* from DFDS. Twelve months later, the 20-year joint ownership agreement between Fred. Olsen and Bergen Line came to an end.

Resulting from this split, the *Jupiter/Black Watch* reverted to Bergen Line but was soon sold to Norway Line for $4.4 million for delivery in October 1986. Following a major refit (which extended her passenger capacity from 750 to 900), she continued with the operation of the Newcastle-Stavanger-Bergen link. Norway Line (by then Color Line) took over all Olsen's North Sea ferry services late in 1990. After a further sale to the Greek company Marlines, sailing as the *Crown*, and a period of serving as an accommodation ship for foreign labour off Dubai, she finally sailed for scrapping in India during 2008.

However, the future of the *Black Prince* lay in quite the opposite direction when she became 100 per cent owned by Fred. Olsen. It was decided to enter the growing cruise business and a complete conversion followed during which time an extra 125 cabins were fitted in the space formerly occupied by the car deck. She

*The unmistakable profile of the **Black Prince** cruising through the Straits of Dover. (FotoFlite)*

reappeared in 1987 as a one-ship cruise line until 1996, when the new *Black Watch* was added to the fleet.

1987 - FROM FERRY TO CRUISE SHIP

Prior to converting the *Black Prince* into a full-time cruise ship, Fred. Olsen Lines commissioned an extensive market research analysis which showed that a change of cruising style might attract new market potential and thereby increase cruise purchasers. A new cruise concept was created and marketed as 'time for a change'.

The *Black Prince*'s original conversion to a cruise ship in 1986-87 was carried out by Wartsila at their Turku yard in Finland and cost NOK 92.5 million, during which time passenger capacity was reduced to between 450 and 500. She was specifically rebuilt with the aim of attracting the younger and sportier end of the market and, to this end, a retractable Marina Park was constructed and stored at the after end of her former vehicle deck. When at anchor,

the stern door would be swung open and the marina/swimming pool would hastily be assembled by the ship's mainly Filipino crew which allowed scuba diving, snorkelling, wind-surfing and water skiing to take place. In addition to these activities, a fitness centre and swimming pool were also built. The ship's maiden voyage in her new role commenced with a 14-day cruise leaving Southampton on 28th February 1987 for Cadiz, Casablanca, the Canary Islands of La Gomera, Tenerife and Lanzarote, Madeira and Gibraltar.

The role of the *Black Prince* in this configuration proved unsuccessful. So Fred. Olsen hastily opted to return her to the ferry trade on a service linking Copenhagen with Gothenburg. Unfortunately, this also proved problematic, mainly due to union objections over her Philippine registry and the employment of foreign crews. A further rethink was therefore required and this was followed by a second refit that was this time aimed at the well-tried, middle-aged, middle class British market. In this role, and with her gross tonnage now increased to 11,209, the ship became an

Top: At the aft end of Deck 6 as the ship lies alongside at Greenock (Glasgow). (John Hendy)

*Above: Thought by some to resemble a Viking helmet, the **Black Prince**'s funnel made her a unique-looking cruise ship. (John Hendy)*

Right: Captain Jan Thommessen ready to take the ship away from the River Clyde in May 2007. (John Hendy)

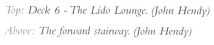

Top: Deck 6 - The Lido Lounge. (John Hendy)

Above: The forward stairway. (John Hendy)

Right: Deck 5 - The elegant Aquitaine Lounge. (John Hendy)

*This stern view of the **Black Prince** shows how the Lido Sun Deck was extended to create a popular seating area and pool over her aft end. (FotoFlite)*

immediate success and very soon gained a loyal following amongst her faithful clientele.

During June 1994, the *Black Prince* attended the fiftieth anniversary commemorations to mark D-Day when she anchored off Omaha Beach before proceeding up the canal to the nearby city of Caen. In view of her size, the *Black Prince*'s annual round of cruises tended to be European-based, the Canaries remaining a firm favourite, although there were the odd sorties to South Africa, the Amazon and the Caribbean while in 2002 she even ran some fly-cruises based in Cuba.

For many years, a happy association existed with the National Trust for Scotland which, between 1984 and 2007, chartered the *Black Prince* for a series of annual themed cruises one of which was always in the Outer Isles. In this role she was ideal with excellent lectures and plenty of Scottish cultural activities. Under their auspices, a retirement cruise on the *Black Prince* took the writer and his wife out to the remote Hebridean outlier of St Kilda where the

ship slowly circumnavigated the archipelago with its towering cliffs and rich abundance of bird life. It was a magical occasion which was made all the more so by the warmth and comfort of the *Black Prince*.

With the arrival of further ships in the Fred. Olsen fleet after 1996, the *Black Prince* was used to test the market in new and untried cruising areas. During the early years of full-time cruising, she had been mainly based in the South of England and worked from Tilbury, Dover and Southampton. However, in 2003 it was decided to offer a limited number of cruises from Leith (Edinburgh) to more northern destinations and their popularity led to more cruises from Dublin, Belfast, Liverpool and Greenock.

ON BOARD

The passenger accommodation on board the *Black Prince* was spread over five decks with the majority of cabins being situated on the Lido Deck (Deck 6), Main Deck (Deck 4) and the Marina

*The **Black Prince** at anchor in Village Bay in the St Kilda archipelago during her Hebridean cruise with the National Trust for Scotland in May and June 2007. (John Hendy)*

Deck (Deck 3 – the former vehicle deck).

Deck 5 was the Lounge Deck on which the majority of public rooms were to be found. At the forward end was the Aquitaine Lounge which was very much in its original condition with plenty of wooden panelling and comfortable armchairs in evidence. Moving towards the stern, the main guest thoroughfare was on the ship's starboard side with firstly the Fleur de Lys Restaurant and then the rather larger Royal Garter Restaurant. At the aft end was the Neptune Lounge which served as the bar and dance floor, and was also the ideal venue for evening lectures and entertainment.

On the deck above (Lido Deck) was the Lido Lounge which acted as an upper floor to the Neptune Lounge and from which one observed the entertainment below. At the aft end of the Lido Deck was the outside Sun Deck and swimming pool. A third restaurant – the Balblom, named after another former Olsen ship, was situated on Deck 7 (Marquee Deck) and acted as an overspill when the ship was busy. Down on Deck 2 was the Sauna Deck, at the aft end of which were found the ship's hairdresser, gymnasium, solarium, massage parlour and inside pool.

Being a former ferry, the *Black Prince* boasted plenty of excellent outside deck space including a magnificent viewing platform immediately above the ship's bridge. Remembering that the *Black Prince* was built for winter passages across the Bay of Biscay, she was also a fine sea-going ship with a beautiful hull line and deep draught which made for a comfortable cruise in all but the worst weathers.

A FOND FAREWELL

The implementation of SOLAS 2010 (Safety of Life at Sea 2010) regulations, sadly brought the *Black Prince*'s long and distinguished career to a close and in this she joined the Cunard liner *Queen Elizabeth 2* which also fell foul of the new regulations. SOLAS 2010 focused principally on the use of combustible materials and, since 2010, no such materials have been permitted anywhere in the construction or conversion of any passenger ship. With knowledge of this impending legislation, Fred. Olsen was quick to announce that the *Black Prince* would cease operations by October 2010. Other veterans were similarly affected and a whole raft of historic cruise ships were sadly withdrawn from active service.

After a series of finales, starting at Liverpool on 9th September 2009 for a 'Round Britain' cruise, the *Black Prince* then undertook a three-night repositioning mini-cruise from the Mersey to

*The **Black Prince** at anchor off Portree in June 2007. (John Hendy)*

Southampton. A ten-night 'Historic Home Ports' cruise – which included a call at Lübeck, where she had been built – was followed by a final 14-night 'Farewell' cruise to the Canaries (where else?) before her return and lay-up on 16th October.

Before setting off to commence her new career, the many historic items associated with Fred. Olsen were carefully removed from the *Black Prince*. Even Kjell Rasmussen's spectacular figurehead of the ballet dancer, Hanne Scram, was craned off and put into storage for future use in the Hvitsten park, where there are now over 30 figureheads displayed, all from Fred. Olsen ships built between 1936 and the early 1970s.

Without doubt, the *Black Prince* was the ship that established Fred. Olsen in the growing cruise trade and her success during the previous 22 years sowed the seeds for the Company we see today. A career lasting 43 years is a remarkable achievement which is unlikely to be repeated.

The *Black Prince* was sold to Servicios Acuaticos De Venezuela (SAVECA) in May 2009 for delivery in November that year and was subsequently renamed *Prince* before sailing to South America. She was later renamed *Ola Esmeralda*, her operators (Ola Cruises) planning to use her for coastal cruising. However, no licence for this was forthcoming and in January 2010, following the Haiti earthquake, she sailed for use as a United Nations accommodation vessel at Port-au-Prince.

Chapter 2

BLACK WATCH

Following an extensive search for a second cruise ship with which to expand their sphere of operations, Fred. Olsen acquired the *Black Watch* in 1996. At this time the cruise industry was expanding and much positive experience with the *Black Prince* indicated that Olsen would have little difficulty in filling a second ship thereby maintaining its place within a buoyant market.

The ship was built in 1972 at the Wartsila New Shipyard in Helsinki for the Royal Viking Line and was originally named *Royal Viking Star*. The brainchild of American businessman Warren Titus, Royal Viking had been formed two years previously and was partly owned by Kloster Cruises, owners of the Norwegian Cruise Line, although each of the three ships was owned by one of the original Norwegian investing partners which – in the case of the 'Star' – was the Bergen Line.

The new ships were as distinctive looking as they were modern and were graced by an extremely raked bow and a tall funnel in the best 'QE2' tradition. As the first of the three new ships, the 21,847-gross-ton *Royal Viking Star* was not identical to her sisters being two feet shorter and with a slightly different interior arrangement. She even boasted a chapel, forward of the theatre, although this feature was not repeated in the subsequent vessels. The ship interiors were designed by the Danish firm of Knud E. Hansen which, over the years has been responsible for many notable vessels.

Until this time the majority of cruising tended to be Caribbean based but Royal Viking saw opportunities to extend this on a world wide basis and ordered the three identical vessels for this purpose. The company hoped to attract wealthy retired people, mainly Americans, and transport them to exotic destinations. Accordingly, these spacious ships carried just 539 passengers, many travelling in suites and staterooms.

The *Royal Viking Star* was the lead ship of the trio and was launched at Helsinki on 12th May 1971. Her patron was the wife of the famous Norwegian explorer Thor Heyerdahl and, after fitting out, the ship sailed to Bergen to be inspected by her owners and for crew familiarisation purposes. During this period Bergen Line's Bergen-Newcastle ferry *Leda* experienced engine troubles, and so the luxurious new cruise ship was pressed into service giving her guests a totally unexpected North Sea crossing in the lap of luxury.

The *Royal Viking Star* finally entered cruise ship service on 26th June 1972. Along with her sisters *Royal Viking Sky* and *Royal Viking Sea*, the ships proved to be an immediate success and were claimed

Top: The **Royal Viking Star**, *as she originally appeared, was one of three sisters.* (FotoFlite)

*Above: A pilot's eye view of the **Black Watch** as she heads out of Dover. (John Mavin)*

Top left: Deck 6 - Braemar Lounge (John Hendy)

Top right: Deck 6 - Braemar Garden Café (John Hendy)

Above left: Deck 6 - Neptune Lounge (John Hendy)

Above right: Deck 6 - Glentanar Restaurant (John Hendy)

Top left: Deck 6 - Orchid Room (John Hendy)

Top right: Deck 6 - stairway (John Hendy)

Above left: Deck 6 - Pipers' Bar (John Hendy)

Above right: Deck 7 - Card Room (John Hendy)

*The **Black Watch** alongside at Dover. (John Hendy)*

BLACK WATCH
NASSAU
7

to be amongst the five most luxurious cruise ships in the world at that time. So popular did they become that, in 1981, the *Royal Viking Star* was sent to Bremerhaven and lengthened by almost 28 metres, which allowed a further 219 guests to be carried. Although making much economic sense, this move did not meet with universal approval, the Norwegian America Line (with which there had been talks involving a possible merger) along with many of the line's clientele fearing that the ships would lose much of their previous exclusivity, ambience and charm. Various other internal modifications took place during this period, including the almost doubling of the ship's restaurant to allow all guests to be accommodated in one sitting. The stretching of the ship saw her gross tonnage rise to 28,221, but the concerns of the Norwegian America Line proved to be well founded and – in an ever-competitive market – it appeared that the three ships had lost something of their previous aristocratic gloss.

The Royal Viking Line had already lost one of its original partners in 1977, when AF Klaveness (owners of the *Royal Viking Sea*) had withdrawn from the group, and unfortunately for Royal Viking Line, increasing operating costs now caused severe financial problems. As a result of this, in 1984 the company and its ships were sold to Kloster Cruises and, in April 1991, the *Royal Viking Star* was transferred to sister company Norwegian Cruise Line and duly renamed *Westward*.

In this role the ship was primarily used for seven-day cruises from New York, Bermuda and the Caribbean and in 1993 accommodation was increased to 850 with the addition of staterooms on the Bridge Deck in the former officers' quarters. A buffet was also added in the lounge on the ship's top deck. Unfortunately, she was not entirely successful in this role, which was somewhat downmarket when compared to the luxury trade that had been her hallmark until this time.

However, in the following year came another switch within the fleet. During April 1994, she was transferred within the group to the Greek-managed Royal Cruise Line and renamed *Star Odyssey* for work based in Vancouver and New York. This phase of her career was to prove all too brief as the Norwegian Cruise Line's parent company (Kloster Cruises) was itself experiencing financial problems which eventually lead to its bankruptcy. The Royal Viking Line was dissolved and the brand was sold to Cunard.

In October 1996, the ship was sold to Fred. Olsen Cruise Lines, which took her over in Piraeus during October 1996 after which she sailed to Southampton for a £4 million refit in readiness for this

*Top: Deck 7 - The Library with the ship model of the former **Black Watch**. (John Hendy)*

Above: Deck 7 - Lido Lounge (John Hendy)

Top left: Deck 7 - the open Promenade Deck (John Hendy)

Top right: Deck 9 - Observatory Lounge (John Hendy)

Above left: Deck 7 - Internet Room (John Hendy)

Above right: Deck 9 - Observatory Lounge (John Hendy)

Top: Deck 5 - shopping arcade (John Hendy)

Above: Deck 3 - Marina Theatre (John Hendy)

Right: Sun Deck - figurehead of the French dramatist Cyrano de Bergerac (John Hendy)

*The graceful lines of the **Black Watch** are very evident in this view of her cruising through the English Channel. (FotoFlite)*

With her bow-thruster pushing her away from the quay at Dover, the **Black Watch** *prepares to head for an Iceland and Greenland cruise. (John Hendy)*

further phase of her career. In the best Fred. Olsen tradition, the ship was renamed *Black Watch* and sailed to Dover for entry into service on 15th November 1996.

The introduction of the *Black Watch* greatly expanded Olsen's worldwide profile and in 2004 she sailed from Southampton on an 'Around the World' voyage, successfully repeating the type of itinerary for which she was originally built. During a rolling period of refurbishment and upgrading, major works were carried out at Hamburg between 18th April and 21st June 2005 when not only was she re-engined and re-propellered but also received a major interior facelift in order to bring her up to the latest cruise ship standards. The installation of new engines was a great success in helping to save on fuel costs.

Amongst the modifications was the dividing of the huge restaurant into two to create the smaller and quieter Orchid Room, alongside the larger Glentanar Restaurant. At the same time, the old chapel was converted into additional cabins.

During the first half of December 2009, the ship underwent a further period of extensive refurbishment back in Hamburg. This involved the reconfiguration of the amidships section on Deck 6 to create a contemporary, casual dining area with 120 seats – the Braemar Garden – and an adjacent 40-seater screened-off area which can also be used for private dining. Other principal areas on the same deck were given new soft furnishings as was the popular Observatory Lounge on Deck 9.

ON BOARD

Now the longest-serving ship in the Fred. Olsen fleet, the

*Fleet companions together at Dover as the **Black Watch** passes the **Braemar**. (John Hendy)*

Black Watch is a much-loved vessel that has gained a tremendous following throughout the years boasting the highest repeat rate amongst her guests of any ship within the fleet, achieving up to 80 per cent repeat custom on some Christmas cruises! When the writer was last on board, the ship was about to leave Dover for a 21-night return cruise to Istanbul and was booked with no fewer than 500 repeat guests. The majority of the cabins are situated on Decks 3, 4 and 5 and have outside views. More spacious and expensive cabins are found on Decks 7, 8 and 9. Deck 3 (Marina Deck) also hosts the Marina Theatre, which seats up to 100 people. It is an ideal venue for lectures and recitals and doubles as a cinema. The ship's Medical Centre is also situated on Deck 3.

Moving up through the ship, Deck 4 (Atlantic Deck) houses the Beauty Salon, while the deck above that (Main Deck) hosts the ship's busy shops, boutiques and Reception Area running along the centre line. Deck 6 (Lounge Deck) is entirely devoted to guest amenities.

Starting at the forward end, the ship's galley opens out into the large Glentanar Restaurant which stretches across the width of the vessel. Leading off this, on the port side, is the oriental-style Orchid Room, serving exactly the same food as the main restaurant, but offering a quieter, more restrained atmosphere.

Moving aft, we enter a further region of the ship that was subject to structural modifications during the 2005 refit. On the port side is the Braemar Garden Café, and in the centre of the ship is the Braemar Garden while on the starboard side is the Braemar Lounge which also serves as a thoroughfare linking the restaurant with the rest of the ship. This leads into the Pipers' Bar, with its Scottish theme throughout (complete with bagpipes), dedicated to the Black Watch Regiment (see page 88), and then the Neptune Lounge – the ship's principal entertainment venue and meeting place for shore excursions. Aft of this is the outside deck with its ample pool and poolside bar.

On Deck 7 (Lido Deck) aft is the Lido Bar, the ship's nightclub which closes every morning at 1am or whenever the last guest retires eventually for the night! Forward of this are two gaming tables (port side) while on the starboard side is the wonderfully appointed Dalreoch Card Room which leads into the Explorers' Library with its semi-circular shelves and comfortable, deep armchairs. A splendid ship's model of the 1938-built *Black Watch* is on display here and paintings and models of past Olsen ships line the walls creating a great sense of the Olsen heritage and echoing the family's contribution to Norway's maritime history. The accommodation on Deck 7 also has a traditional wood-floored open promenade circumnavigating it and for the fitter guests, the popular five-circuit walk equates to one mile.

Deck 8 is the Bridge Deck on which it is possible to approach the bridge wings to observe the vessel being manoeuvred in and out of port. Otherwise, this deck is devoted to cabins.

The Observatory Lounge on Deck 9 (Marquee Deck) surely boasts the best vistas in the ship. The room is predominately blue in colour, which gives a cool feeling in an otherwise warm space. Excellent views are possible through the floor to ceiling panoramic windows, and it is always well worth the effort to seek it out and enjoy the unrivalled views that it provides – as well as the fine selection of cocktails! At the aft end of this deck is another pool with adjacent Jacuzzis and bar.

The Sun Deck (Deck 10) speaks for itself and is devoted entirely to leisure activities. The well-stocked gymnasium and fitness centre are situated on this deck – complete with sauna – while above this are golf nets and even a tennis court.

As with all Fred. Olsen cruise ships, there's something for everyone! There is little doubt that the *Black Watch* is both a stately and extremely well-built ship and has retained many of the traditional internal fixtures that have helped give her such a following amongst cruise guests. She retains her classic profile and, like all Olsen vessels, she is impeccably maintained and is a credit to her Master and crew.

Top: The **Black Watch** *manoeuvring in Dover Harbour. (John Mavin)*

Above: *'Lit up' in port before the start of another cruise. (John Mavin)*

Chapter 3

BRAEMAR

The 19,089-gross-ton *Braemar* was built by the Union Navale de Levante of Valencia, Spain in 1993. Originally constructed as the second of a pair of vessels for Effjohn's Crown Cruise Line and named *Crown Dynasty*, the ship was named by Mrs Betty Ford, the wife of the then-President of the United States, and spent her early career cruising for the American market. Unfortunate financial problems soon saw the company taken over by Commodore Cruise Line which in the following year entered into a marketing agreement with Cunard Line when the ship was briefly named *Cunard Crown Dynasty* for weekly cruises to the Caribbean.

In 1997, the ship passed to Majesty Cruise Line and became the *Crown Majesty*, but after one season was taken by Norwegian Cruise Line and was renamed *Norwegian Dynasty*. In this guise, the ship cruised for a further two years before being returned to her resurrected original owners, operating with her original name in 1999 and sailing from the US ports of Philadelphia and Baltimore.

This was not a particularly auspicious start for what was still a comparatively new ship and following the bankruptcy of Commodore Cruise Line, she was again advertised for sale early in 2001.

For some time Fred. Olsen Cruise Lines had been looking for a suitable vessel to become its third cruise ship and with her shallow draught, this modern ship would allow visits to many places that the ever-growing Noah's Arks of the cruise ship world would be unable able to enter. The vessel presented a very modern and sleek profile and her lines carried something of the yacht about them. Her light and open interior, crowned by an extremely impressive atrium, rising through five decks, made her an ideal Caribbean cruise ship. With expansion in the air, the ship was acquired by Fred. Olsen and named *Braemar*.

The ship was promptly sent to Blohm & Voss in Hamburg for an extensive refit; as she had originally been designed for seven-day cruises, the work included enlarging both her fuel and water tanks to make her more suitable for the type of work Fred. Olsen envisaged. During the refit, certain artefacts from Fred. Olsen's first *Braemar* (1953-1975) were given to the ship thereby giving her the sense of continuity that Fred. Olsen has always sought to provide on board its vessels.

With the work duly completed and the ship now internally highly recognisable as a Fred. Olsen vessel, the *Braemar* entered service on 11th August 2001, operating a Scandinavian cruise from Dover. During the passage northwards, the ship docked at Dundee to

Top: The ship's bridge on Deck 7. (John Hendy)

*Above: The **Braemar's** new 31.2 metre section ready to be inserted into her hull during May 2008. (Marko Stampehl)*

Top: Deck 5 - Braemar Club (John Hendy)

Above: Deck 5 - Coral Club (John Hendy)

Right: Deck 4 - the ship's impressive atrium (John Hendy)

Morning Light Pub (John Hendy)

Deck 5 - Library (John Hendy)

Deck 5 - Neptune Lounge (John Hendy)

Top left: Deck 5 - Reception (John Hendy)

Top right: Deck 7 - Skylark Club (John Hendy)

Above: Deck 6 - Palms Café (John Hendy)

Right: Deck 8 - Grampian Restaurant (John Hendy)

allow guests time ashore to visit the Highland village, close to Balmoral, after which she had been named.

The *Braemar* immediately gave Fred. Olsen a firm foothold in a totally new market and was primarily used during the winter months for long distance fly-cruises which were very much a 'first' for Fred. Olsen. Whereas the majority of cruises had previously started and ended in UK ports, the *Braemar* allowed guests to fly to the Caribbean (usually Barbados), cruise in the West Indies or even up the River Amazon as far as Manaus, before returning by air. During the summer, it was back to the UK where her cruises tended to be directed towards the Norwegian fjords and the Baltic capitals.

In May to June 2008 the *Braemar* was returned to Hamburg where she was lengthened by 31.2 metres thereby increasing her guest capacity by 250 to 986 and her gross tonnage to 24,344. At this time, Deck 8 gained a forward Observatory Lounge, a traditional 'Morning Light' British pub, an extra restaurant and an arts and crafts room, while the extra outside deck space that the pre-built insertion gave, provided an extended Lido and outside swimming pool.

The *Braemar* duly arrived at Hamburg on 13th May 2008 and entered the Elbe 17 dry dock to be cut in half. The new midships section was constructed at nearby Bremerhaven and had arrived in Hamburg under tow on 6th April. With the 1,200 metres of steel cutting to divide the ship completed, the new section was inserted on 21st May and three days later, the work began to weld all three sections together. The work required tremendous skill and pin-point accuracy on the part of the Blohm & Voss team and it was of great credit to them that the job was completed on time.

The work successfully completed, the *Braemar* then sailed to the Mediterranean for a series of summer fly-cruises based on the port of Civitavecchia (Rome) while that winter she was based in Miami (Florida). During her first season in operation as a stretched ship, it was found that her extra length had actually improved her seakeeping qualities.

Unfortunately, the economic downturn saw the winter fly-cruise trade cease at the close of the 2011-2012 season, with Fred. Olsen citing the high cost of flights as their reason for doing so. For the foreseeable future, the *Braemar* will concentrate on year-round UK-based cruises.

ON BOARD

Passenger accommodation is spread across seven decks and

Top: Deck 8 - Observatory Lounge (John Hendy)

Above: Deck 8 - aft stairway (John Hendy)

The **Braemar's** spacious outside decks enable great views; here, of Dover Castle. (John Hendy)

Deck 8 - Sun Deck (John Hendy)

*The **Braemar** leaving Dover for a cruise to the Canary Islands. (John Hendy)*

BRAEMAR

apart from on Deck 5 (Lounge Deck) which is entirely devoted to guest amenities, the principal public rooms are mainly found at the ship's after end.

Deck 8 (Marquee Deck) houses the Grampian Restaurant (aft), with its calm and peaceful ambience and restrained colour palette. Outside, forward of the funnel, the open central deck area boasts twin swimming pools, a children's paddling pool and Jacuzzis. The banks of sheltered and shaded sun beds are particularly popular in the Caribbean and the attractive pool bar is particularly busy serving the numerous sun lovers. At the forward end of the open deck, twin flights of steps lead to the deck area above which is not only used for a golf driving range but also gives an unimpeded view on top of the Observatory Lounge – an excellent place to be when arriving or leaving port. Below this area on Deck 8 is the relaxing ship's Observatory Lounge which is sited above the bridge and which, through its full-length panoramic windows, gives excellent forward views across the bow. Although smaller than other such rooms in the rest of the fleet, it is both a popular and intimate space.

Deck 7 (Bridge Deck) hosts the informal Skylark Bar, complete with gaming tables. This area has a very contemporary feel, with bright furniture, window blinds and carpets and modern paintings lining the walls. Adjacent to this is the Crafts Room, a popular addition to the ship since her stretching in 2008.

Deck 6 (Lido Deck) is home to the Lido Bar and Palms Café which is a busy meeting place when guests prefer to eat informally rather than visiting either of the ship's restaurants. It very much captures the atmosphere of a traditional Caribbean beachside café with its bright mural, the use of mock wooden beams, simple furniture and scattered pot plants.

Deck 5 (Lounge Deck) is the main guest deck and boasts a host of comfortable seating areas to suit all moods and tastes. From Deck 7 downwards, the ship's aft decks all offer generous and sheltered outside seating, cascading down towards Deck 5 which offers the largest of these areas. Entering the accommodation at this point, the Coral Club's seating is arranged around a small performance/dance area which is very popular during the evenings. Moving forward we pass by the ship's main Reception desk (with its fine model of the ship before she was stretched), shops and boutiques and the cruise sales and tours offices. The passageway then passes through the Braemar Club, a relaxing seated area, complete with modern artwork and tartan carpet, off which are the Internet Room, Card Room and well-stocked ship's Library with its quiet and restful atmosphere. Another fine ship's model is on display

*The **Braemar** is the only ship within the fleet permitting access to the fo'c'sle. (John Hendy)*

in the Braemar Club; this is a builder's model of Olsen's North Sea ferry *Braemar* of 1953, which survived on the Oslo/Kristiansand-Newcastle route until 1975, by which time she was the very last traditional North Sea passenger ship in service.

Further forward, the Morning Light Pub displays the tradition and intimacy of a commodious and cosy English public house lounge bar with its deeply upholstered leather settees and armchairs. The walls are lined with shipping ephemera from Olsen's past giving the room a rich nautical atmosphere. This nautical theme is continued throughout the ship, with many historical paintings of early Olsen ships, both sail and steam-driven.

At the forward end is the ship's theatre, the Neptune Lounge which hosts the main entertainment with a variety of shows, lectures and recitals. It also serves as the meeting point for all shore excursions before they leave the ship.

In addition, Deck 5 offers a complete outside circuit of the ship and is therefore popular with walkers and joggers, also affording guests access to the fo'c'sle – the outside deck forward of the bridge. This is a unique public area within the fleet and allows the unusual opportunity of walking right to the ship's bow in the manner of the stars in the film 'Titanic'!

The *Braemar*'s comfortable main restaurant – The Thistle Restaurant – is situated aft on Deck 4. Immediately forward of this is the ship's atrium which rises up through five decks and allows light to flood into the accommodation, giving this intimate cruise ship the feel of the big liner.

The decks below are mainly fitted with cabins although Deck 3 (Atlantic Deck) is fitted with the Fitness Centre and the Health & Beauty Salon, while Deck 2 (Marina Deck) houses the Medical Centre and launderette.

The *Braemar* has a cosy and intimate feel about her and although dwarfed by many of today's vast and box-like cruise ships, her size and simple layout soon allow guests to find their way about with ease enabling them to enjoy all the comforts and facilities expected in this first class floating hotel.

*Dawn arrival as the **Braemar** swings off her berth at Dover. (John Mavin)*

Chapter 4

BOUDICCA

The early history of the *Boudicca* closely mirrors that of her sister ship *Black Watch*. The 21,891 gross ton vessel was built at Wartsila's New Shipyard in Helsinki as the *Royal Viking Sky*, the second of a trio of luxury cruise ships constructed for the fledgling Royal Viking Line, under the wing of Kloster Cruises. The ship was launched on 25th May 1972 and after fitting out was duly delivered to her Norwegian owners, Det Nordenfjeldske D/S of Trondheim on the following 5th June.

As with her sister ships, there followed a successful series of luxury world cruises for as few as 550 wealthy guests. However, in order to increase capacity, she sailed to Bremerhaven in 1982, where she was stretched by almost 28 metres raising her gross tonnage to 28,078. This allowed for a further 200 guests to be accommodated and necessitated the doubling in size of the dining room in order to seat them all in a single sitting. The stretching of all three 'Royal Viking' ships was seen as a cheaper alternative to building a fourth vessel although unfortunately, following the modifications, many previously loyal guests felt that the ships had lost a degree of their previous intimacy and began to look elsewhere for their cruises.

After the Kloster Group had acquired the Royal Viking Line business outright during 1984, seven years later the *Royal Viking Sky* was renamed *Sunward* after transferring to the Norwegian Cruise Line. In this role she operated short cruises from Miami to the Bahamas and, reflecting her new American clientele, was duly fitted with a casino, video arcade and a children's playroom. For a ship designed to carry the rich and wealthy on high class 'Around the World' cruises, this was something of a fall from grace and there followed a peripatetic, 14-year period during which she was switched from operator to operator before eventually finding stability with Fred. Olsen.

At this point in her career her story differs from that of the *Black Watch* as in 1992 she was sold to Birka Cruises (based in the Aland Islands) and renamed *Birka Queen* for short, duty-free cruises in the Baltic Sea. These proved unsuccessful and so later that year she was chartered back to her former owners and resumed the name of *Sunward*.

Following refurbishment, during 1993 she was again chartered, this time to Princess Cruises, and became their *Golden Princess* for use on summer Alaska and winter Mexican cruises from San Francisco and Los Angeles. This was very much a stopgap role, for as soon as Princess Cruises introduced larger tonnage, the charter

*Top: The **Boudicca** was originally the **Royal Viking Sky**. (FotoFlite)*

*Above: Seen in the River Elbe, the **Boudicca** approaches the German port of Hamburg. (Marko Stampehl)*

*The **Boudicca** at Gudvangen at the end of Naeroyfjord - a favourite destination for cruise ships. (Bruce Peter)*

Top left: Deck 5 - Reception Area (John Hendy)

Top right: Deck 6 - Four Seasons Restaurant (John Hendy)

Above: Deck 6 - Iceni Room (John Hendy)

Right: Deck 6 - Heligan Room (John Hendy)

Deck 6 - seating area adjacent to the Secret Garden Café (John Hendy)

Deck 6 - Neptune Bar (John Hendy)

Deck 6 - Secret Garden Café (John Hendy)

of the *Golden Princess* was terminated and she was returned to Birka Cruises in 1996.

Birka Cruises now sold its ship on to Star Cruises of Malaysia who renamed her *SuperStar Capricorn*. Following another refit, this time to adapt her to the Asian market, she was used on short cruises from Taiwan across the East China Sea to the Japanese island of Okinawa. A further charter followed in 1998, this time to Hyundai Merchant Marine for a series of highly ambitious cruises between South and North Korea. In this guise she was renamed *Hyundai Keumgang* but the political climate was not yet right for such a challenging venture and on its failure in November 2001, the ship was returned to Star Cruises, regaining her former name, and was promptly laid up.

Her Asian ownership over, a further sale occurred in 2004, this time to Spanish owners Iberojet for Barcelona-based Mediterranean cruising under the name of *Grand Latino*. Although yet another expensive refit took place, again the venture failed and with the ship returned to the sales market, in the following year she was duly purchased by Fred. Olsen.

Olsen had once again been searching the sales market for a further ship to expand its ever-popular brand of cruising, and the appearance of this ship was an opportunity not to be missed. Sister ship *Black Watch* had already proved herself to be ideal both in terms of size and layout. Although the new ship had experienced a rather peripatetic recent career, a series of expensive refits ensured that she was in good mechanical and structural order, and she proved to be the perfect addition to the fleet. The ship was renamed *Boadicea* (later revised to the alternative spelling 'Boudicca') becoming Olsen's fourth cruise ship and happily rejoining her erstwhile sister, *Black Watch*. The choice of name was a 'first' for Fred. Olsen, but served to underline its commitment to the British market.

Olsen lost no time in sending the new purchase to the Blohm & Voss shipyard in Hamburg in December 2005 for re-engining and complete refurbishment. A number of modifications took place to the ship's guest accommodation; the once huge dining area was made into three separate restaurants while the lower theatre area was converted into extra state rooms and a Fitness Centre. Of particular merit was a new Deck 6 buffet restaurant named The Secret Garden. The ship's interior reflected her varied career and changes of ownership which had managed to produce quite a different layout to that of her sister, the *Black Watch*. The *Boudicca* now boasted a thoroughly modern and contemporary interior

Top: Deck 6 - Tintagel Restaurant (John Hendy)

Above: Deck 8 - the ship's bridge. (John Hendy)

Deck 7 - Library (John Hendy)

Deck 7 - Lido Lounge (John Hendy)

Deck 9 - Observatory Lounge (John Hendy)

which was unmistakably Olsen in its completion yet displayed the styles and expectations of the first decade of the 21st century.

The refitting work complete, the *Boudicca*'s first cruise for Fred. Olsen was from Dover to the Canaries on 25th February 2006. Following the withdrawal from service of the *Black Prince* in 2009, the *Boudicca* was transferred northwards in March 2010 to operate cruises from Liverpool, Greenock, Rosyth and Newcastle.

On return from her Christmas Canary Island cruise, during early January 2011, the *Boudicca* entered dry dock in Hamburg for a period of further refurbishment. A key element of the work involved the relocation of the Fitness Centre, previously situated on Deck 4 (Atlantic Deck), up to the top of the ship on Deck 10 (Sun Deck) in the same position as on board her sister ship, *Black Watch*. The removal of the Fitness Centre created space for 17 new cabins while the refit also saw the replacement of the last of the Company's open lifeboats. Significant investment was made in four new, enclosed lifeboats and two rescue boats, which represented an important upgrade in this area.

Following her refit, the *Boudicca* resumed service on 16th January 2011, with a 14-night cruise to the Canaries from Southampton.

ON BOARD

As previously mentioned, although the *Black Watch* and *Boudicca* started their careers as sister ships, there are now marked internal differences between them. As the *Boudicca* is the most recent addition to the Fred. Olsen fleet of the two, her public rooms are more contemporary in style without ever losing that essential ambience for which the Company is renowned.

The majority of cabins are situated on Decks 3, 4 and 5, with the Medical Centre forward on Deck 3 and the Beauty Salon and Sauna and Steam Rooms on Deck 4. Deck 5 houses the ship's Reception Area and shops along with the Photo Gallery and the Future and Shore Tours Offices. These are situated along the ship's centre line and form a busy arcade through the forward part of the ship.

Deck 6 (Lounge Deck) is entirely devoted to public rooms and thus is the centre of the ship's life and operations. At the forward end is the ship's galley (kitchen) which leads into three quite separate and distinctive restaurants. On the port (left) side are the Heligan Room and Tintagel Restaurant while on the starboard side of the ship is the Four Seasons Restaurant which mirrors the Tintagel Restaurant.

The aft end of Deck 6 looking forward. The figurehead on display was originally on the **Baldrian** *of 1947. (John Hendy)*

Deck 9 - Observatory Lounge (John Hendy)

*Surrounded by steep mountains, the **Boudicca** is seen alongside at Flaam which lies on a tributary of the 204 km long Sognefjord. (Bruce Peter)*

*The **Boudicca** at sea showing her extensive outside deck area at the stern. (FotoFlite)*

Inboard from the Heligan Room is the Secret Garden Café surrounded by its delicate and pierced wooden Chinese Chippendale style screens very much creating the appearance of a mystical and secretly enclosed space. If required the screens can be folded back to make one large and comfortable area stretching across the width of the ship. Moving aft is the bar with its cosy lounges either side. A grand piano provides relaxing music at busy times helping to provide the palm court experience of a spacious and luxurious hotel foyer.

Moving down the ship's port side, the Neptune Bar leads into the Neptune Lounge, the principal entertainment area and meeting place for shore excursions. The Neptune Bar is mirrored on the starboard side by the Iceni Room, which was refurbished in mid 2010 to provide a dedicated tea/coffee station. The upward slope in floor levels in these two rooms allows the Neptune Lounge to offer tiered seating, so that everyone enjoys a good view of the central stage area.

The outside aft end of Deck 6 contains the swimming pool, Jacuzzis and the adjacent poolside buffet. The aft end of Deck 7 (Lido Deck) houses the relaxing and informal Lido Lounge, with its adjacent gaming tables. Forward of this is the excellently appointed ship's Library, the books themselves housed in a semi-circular series of shelves (as on all four Fred. Olsen ships); of particular note is the specially made table in the Library, featuring a collaboration between Fred. Olsen and the Colchester and Ipswich Museum Service, showcasing the important Roman heritage of the UK's oldest recorded Roman town, sacked by the British Queen Boudicca during her ultimately ill-fated revolt against Roman rule. The Library's deep and comfortable armchairs allow guests to take in the panoramic views of the changing seascape at their leisure. Here, and throughout the ship, are examples of carefully chosen contemporary artwork which assist in the creation of a thoroughly modern and yet tasteful interior. The adjacent Card Room has one wall covered in shields and plaques which are presented to the ship whenever she makes a 'maiden' call at a new port. The compact Internet Room is situated a little further forward on the port side.

Deck 7 offers an open promenade around which guests can enjoy a complete circuit of the ship – five circuits equate to one mile. The forward view overlooks the ship's fo'c'sle, complete with its deck cranes, winches, capstans and the crew's swimming pool.

Deck 8 is the Bridge Deck containing guest cabins while the Marquee Deck (Deck 9) houses the attractive Observatory Lounge at its forward end. This is an excellent and relaxing space to enjoy spare time with wonderful all-round views of the sea or whichever port the ship happens to be visiting. At the after end of this deck are the Marquee Pool and its adjacent bar while Deck 10 (Sun Deck) is home to the sparkling new Fitness Centre and Gymnasium and golf nets.

The *Boudicca* is a beautifully appointed vessel. Her interior is both comfortable and modern with many fine examples of contemporary artwork to admire and which help create an ambience which is both unique to the ship and yet quintessentially Fred. Olsen Cruise Lines in character.

The third of the original trio of Royal Viking ships was *the Royal Viking Sea*. This ship presently operates for the German cruise company Phoenix Reisen and sails as the *Albatros*. Of the three Royal Viking ships, her interior has probably changed the least.

*The **Boudicca** is followed out of harbour by the Dover pilot boat. (John Mavin)*

Chapter 5

BALMORAL

Fred. Olsen's motor vessel *Balmoral* was originally built at Jos. L. Meyer's Papenburg yard in Germany as the *Crown Odyssey*. She was launched in November 1987 for service with the Greek-owned, American-financed Royal Cruise Line of Piraeus, and many of her internal glass doors retain their original crown motif to this day.

As built, the ship measured 217.9 metres with a 28.2-metre beam and a 6.8 metre draught. Her lines were fairly typical of that period and she boasted a handsome, if rather exaggerated, bow, compact lines and a transom stern. At 34,242 gross tons, the ship was capable of cruising at speeds of up to 22.5 knots, her four MAK diesels developing 21,300 kW. Guest accommodation was usually for 1,104, although a maximum of 1,230 could be carried.

The *Crown Odyssey* was delivered during June 1988 and operated her first cruise between Emden and Tilbury. Two years later she was reflagged in the Bahamas and was sold to Kloster Cruises in 1992. In May 1995, she became the *Norwegian Crown* for their Norwegian Cruise Line but five years later reverted to *Crown Odyssey* for service with subsidiary company, Orient Line. With this completed, the vessel was again renamed *Norwegian Crown* whilst undergoing refit in Singapore. The Fitness Centre was added above the bridge in this period.

Looking to further expand its fleet, Fred. Olsen purchased the

*The **Balmoral** was originally the **Crown Odyssey** and is seen leaving Dover as the **Norwegian Crown**. (FotoFlite)*

vessel in 2006 for delivery in the following November and, after being taken over in New York on 5th November 2007, she duly arrived for major surgery at Blohm & Voss in Hamburg on 16th November. The project had actually commenced in July when work had started on building the new 30-metre section at Schichau Seebeck at Bremerhaven. This was launched on 6th October, and

*The **Balmoral** undergoing stretching at Blohm & Voss, Hamburg, during late 2008. (Blohm & Voss)*

The **Balmoral** approaching the White Cliffs of Dover. (FotoFlite)

towed sideways to Hamburg where it arrived at the end of October.

The yet-to-be-renamed *Norwegian Crown* duly arrived at Hamburg's Elbe 17 dry dock on 16th November and cutting her in half commenced two days later. This completed, the two sections were pulled apart on 21st November and within 48 hours, the new section was in the process of being inserted before the lengthened ship was welded back together again. This was the most ambitious refit and redesign programme ever undertaken by Fred. Olsen, the 30-metre section giving the stretched ship an extra 186 guest cabins. The stretching involved the installation of some 160 kilometres of new cable within the ship and a total 'cutting length' of 1,500 metres.

In keeping with the Olsen nomenclature, the lengthened ship was named *Balmoral*; gross tonnage was raised to 43,537 and guest numbers to 1,350.

The *Balmoral* duly arrived at Dover on 23rd January 2008 to carry out her maiden voyage on 30th January but in spite of the valiant efforts of all concerned, the ambitious time scale given to refurbish the ship's interior completely was not sufficient and so sadly her first cruise with Fred. Olsen had to be postponed. Instead she sailed for Southampton where the work was finished. She eventually arrived back at Dover on 13th February when, following a firework send off and a carnival atmosphere on board, she sailed that evening for the West Indies.

With such an iconic name as *Balmoral*, even before stepping on board, her guests would surely have made associations with traditional furnishings combined with the comforts of a capacious Scottish country mansion in the best baronial style. As with all Fred. Olsen ships, the *Balmoral* is unashamedly British in character. Her fittings are restrained and easy on the eye, she is both quiet in nature and quiet in character with much use having been made of browns and greens to create a restful and peaceful environment in which to enjoy a cruise. Her subdued interior is quite unlike the more recently built floating cruise resorts of the 'bling' generation with futuristic interiors, bright lights and music pounding on every deck and in every bar. It is therefore hardly surprising that the general perception of all Fred. Olsen vessels is that they are directed at attracting the more mature end of the market.

ON BOARD

The *Balmoral* is by far the largest vessel in the Fred. Olsen fleet

Top left: Deck 6 - Art Gallery leading to the Ballindalloch Restaurant (John Hendy)

Top right: Cruising in the Kiel Canal en route for the Baltic (John Hendy)

Above: Deck 7 - the recently inserted outside deck area (John Hendy)

Right: Deck 11 - looking forward (John Hendy)

Deck 7 - Palms Café (John Hendy)

Deck 7 - a corner of the Morning Light Pub (John Hendy)

Deck 7 - looking down into the Reception Area on Deck 6 (John Hendy)

and yet, such is her design, that she retains the intimacy and friendliness of her smaller companions. Her size allows for more of the same on a larger scale and although she boasts guest accommodation for as many as 1,350, she hides that number well so that she never gives the impression of being busy or full.

Guest accommodation on the *Balmoral* stretches between Decks 3 and 11 with crew cabins down below the water line on Deck 2. Deck 7 (Lounge Deck) is entirely devoted to public guest spaces whilst other principal guest areas are mainly situated towards the ship's stern.

The *Balmoral*'s eating areas are clustered at her after end with the principal Ballindalloch Restaurant being situated on Deck 6 (Main Deck). This impressive area stretches across the width of the ship, and contains the eye-catching central Tiffany-style illuminated ceiling although this is certainly not the only place in which such an effect has been created in the ship. The corridor leading forward from the Ballindalloch Restaurant houses the attractive ship's Art Gallery through which one passes to reach the main Reception Area with its offices for shore tours, Customer Relations office and Port Shop.

With the increase of guests following the ship's stretching, extra mirror-image restaurants were created on Deck 10 with the Avon Restaurant on the starboard side and Spey Restaurant on the port side. Again a cool palette has been used to decorate these rooms, giving the effect of delightful airy interiors.

For those guests preferring a less formal setting, the Palms Café on Deck 7 is a large and popular area at lunch and tea times. On the deck above aft are the Lido Lounge and bar, which spills out onto the open deck overlooking one of the ship's two swimming pools. The Lido Bar is housed within a large 'glass house' of recent construction.

The main entertainment area is the Neptune Lounge, forward on Deck 7. This comfortable theatre, with its tiered seating, is the centre for the evening shows, lectures and recitals as well as the morning meeting place for shore excursions. Evening shows are split into two sittings in order to coincide with meal times.

Between the Palms Café (aft) and the forward Neptune Lounge, Deck 7 also contains the comfortable Morning Light Pub. With its deep settees and nautical memorabilia it exudes the atmosphere of a cosy British seaside public house. In the *Balmoral*'s newly inserted section, the spacious Library, with its wonderful sailing ship model and deep sea-facing armchairs is a popular place for a quiet read or simply somewhere to relax during time at

Top: Deck 7 - Morning Light Pub (John Hendy)

Above: Deck 7 - Neptune Lounge (John Hendy)

Deck 11 - Observatory Lounge (John Hendy)

Deck 10 - Spey Restaurant (John Hendy)

Deck 6 - Ballindalloch Restaurant (John Hendy)

Leaving Helsinki (John Hendy)

*The **Balmoral** alongside at Tallinn (Estonia) (John Hendy)*

Fred. Olsen Cruise Lines

sea. The adjacent Card Room and Internet Room (all port side) and the Braemar Lounge (starboard side) are all situated nearby.

Forward of this is the main Reception Area and atrium which links Deck 6 with Deck 7 and around which all the ship's offices and retail areas are situated. This is truly the ship's 'Piccadilly Circus' and although located along the central thoroughfare, careful use has been made of bright reflective surfaces and open stairs, in order to create a greater sense of light and space. An excellent model of the *Balmoral* is displayed on Deck 7.

The bridge is situated on Deck 9 and above this is the Beauty Salon and Fitness Centre. Although added before Fred. Olsen took over the ship, this space possibly has the best views on board with magnificent forward vistas.

The top deck is Deck 11 (Marquee Deck) on which guests may walk around the funnel, relax on sun beds behind glass screens or make use of the ship's second pool. Forward is the Observatory Lounge and Marquee Bar where nightclub-style piano music is played during the evenings, and which proves to be a very relaxing after dinner area to sit and chat. Although the large floor-to-ceiling panoramic windows can create a warm environment during the day, the blue carpet (with its nautical anchor and compass design) creates a cool ambience in which to enjoy the passing seascape.

For those guests who like to enjoy uninterrupted views of the sea, the after end of Deck 11 proves ideal and an uninterrupted forward view can be gained. Deck 7 provides a pleasant promenade around the bridge front and below the lifeboats, where four complete circuits of this deck equate to one mile.

The *Balmoral* is a beautifully maintained vessel and there is always plenty of evidence of ongoing maintenance in order to keep the ship in immaculate condition. Her paintwork is inevitably spotless and the varnished rails are beautifully kept, as are her teak decks.

Although the *Balmoral* is by far the largest vessel in the Fred. Olsen fleet, she is not so large as to lose that vital intimate ingredient which the company works so hard both to achieve and foster. She is a ship with an excellent range of facilities and spaciousness, and whilst on a Baltic cruise in June 2010, the writer found the whole on-board experience both wonderfully relaxing and escapist. On his birthday, he was even serenaded by the splendid Mahesh and his stewards during dinner in the Spey Restaurant!

Chapter 6

FRED. OLSEN's CHARITABLE CAUSES

red. Olsen is renowned for its friendly, personable approach to cruising, and this passion for being a 'human scale' company is mirrored in the cruise line's support for a number of important and meaningful charitable causes.

FRED. OLSEN AND THE RNLI

Fred. Olsen's guests have been raising funds for the Royal National Lifeboat Institution (RNLI) on board its cruise ships since the 1960s, when RNLI volunteers, Mr and Mrs Howard Bell, started the initiative to encourage fellow guests to help the charity to save lives at sea. The relationship has grown ever since, and Fred. Olsen is now the RNLI's longest-running corporate partner.

Fred. Olsen has been involved in shipping since 1848 and so the links with the RNLI are an important part of the cruise line's seafaring tradition. The Company prides itself on providing a very personal service across its fleet and fundraising for the RNLI has become an institution on all its ships.

During its long-running association with the RNLI, the generous donations of Fred. Olsen's guests have funded no fewer than four inshore lifeboats. In addition to this three mobile training units, three seminar rooms at the Lifeboat College in Poole in Dorset and the development and funding of three drive-on, drive-off lifeboat launching trolleys at Mudeford, Cullercoats and Criccieth have also been funded.

In late 2011, the RNLI launched the fourth inshore lifeboat funded by Fred. Olsen's guests - an Atlantic 85, costing £180,000 - in the Kyle of Lochalsh, in the highlands of Scotland.

The name that was chosen for the new inshore lifeboat - nominated by Karen Potter, a guest on board *Black Watch* - is *Spirit of Fred. Olsen*. The lifeboat can accommodate four crew, with an enlarged space for casualties, and is capable of speeds of up to 35 Knots. The RNLI said: "We are immensely proud of the partnership between Fred. Olsen Cruise Lines and the RNLI, which has been built up over the last 40 years. The new Kyle of Lochalsh lifeboat *Spirit of Fred. Olsen* really highlights this, and the tremendous amount of fundraising that takes place on board Fred. Olsen's cruise ships, which is so valuable to the Charity."

The new Kyle lifeboat replaces the previous Atlantic 75 class boat, called *Alexander Cattanach*, which had been stationed at Kyle since 1997. Kyle launched 14 times in 2011, and in 2010 it was the 12th busiest station in Scotland, with 24 launches.

*Top: The **Spirit of Fred. Olsen** working near the Kyle of Lochalsh. (RNLI)*

Above: In May 2010, HRH Prince Michael of Kent (left) presented Mike Rodwell, Managing Director of Fred. Olsen Cruise Lines, with the RNLI's 'Lifetime Achievement Award'. (Fred. Olsen Cruise Lines)

No 3 Guard, The Black Watch 3rd Battalion, The Royal Regiment of Scotland, at the Aberfeldy Memorial in 2009.

In May 2010, Fred. Olsen was presented with a 'Lifetime Achievement Award' by Royal Patron H.R.H. Prince Michael of Kent in recognition of its ongoing commitment, at the RNLI's annual awards ceremony at the Barbican Centre, London.

FRED. OLSEN AND THE BLACK WATCH REGIMENT

When people think of Fred. Olsen, they often conjure up an image of the ever-popular *Black Watch*, the 'Grande Dame' of the fleet. It is because of this connection that Fred. Olsen has teamed up with The Black Watch Museum Trust which aims to celebrate and sustain the unique heritage and tradition of The Black Watch Regiment at Balhousie Castle, near Perth, its historic home. Fred. Olsen customers will be aware of the Olsen family's passion for Scotland, with some of the names on board: Balmoral,

*The ever-popular **Black Watch** slips away from Dover at the start of another cruise. (John Hendy)*

Another of the Company's fine figureheads is displayed on board the **Braemar**. *(John Hendy)*

See how they grow: from left to right - the **Black Prince**, **Black Watch** *and* **Balmoral** *alongside at Tenerife. (Fred. Olsen Cruise Lines)*

Glentanar, and Ballindalloch to name but a few.

Disbanded in the Government's 2006 reorganisation of the Army, the Black Watch Regiment is one of the world's most famous fighting units. Along the way, The Black Watch collected an incredible 164 battle honours, 14 VCs and a reputation that places the Regiment in a category of its own.

Fred. Olsen has linked up with The Black Watch Museum Trust to promote the famous name and keep the heritage of The Black Watch Regiment alive. Guests on board all four Fred. Olsen ships will find leaflets in their cabins giving details of the aims of the Trust outlining the fundraising plans for the Castle and inviting them to become Friends of The Black Watch Castle and Museum and help to support this important military institution.

The Black Watch Heritage Appeal was launched in September 2008. Its aim was to raise in excess of £3.2 million to provide a permanent home for the Museum and archive in Perth, the historic centre of the Regimental recruiting area. This enabled The Black Watch Museum Trust to purchase Balhousie Castle, which became its property in December 2008. It has also enabled detailed building plans to be commissioned. The Museum houses unique and special collections, illustrating two-and-a-half centuries of the treasures of Scotland's oldest Highland Regiment, including uniforms, fine paintings, medals, photographs, weapons,

*The **Black Prince** leads her fleet companions **Braemar** and **Balmoral** into the Norwegian port of Bergen. (Fred. Olsen Cruise Lines)*

military equipment and dioramas, all of which bring to life the proud military heritage of this family regiment.

Fred. Olsen is also working with The Black Watch Museum Trust in other ways to promote the Regiment, such as through an updated exhibition of military regalia on board the *Black Watch*.

THE COMPANY HOUSE FLAG

The distinctive blue and white pennant was designed for Fred. Olsen by the secretary of the Norwegian Yacht Club. It was with this flag that Olsen won the Kiel Regatta in 1895 in his yacht *Storegut*. Deciding that it represented a strong symbol of speed and dependability, the pennant first appeared on Olsen's first steam ship, the *Bayard* in 1910 and has happily been used ever since.

The distinctive blue and white pennant of Fred.Olsen Cruise Lines.

Chapter 7

THE FLEET

Tony Rive

Tony Rive

BLACK WATCH

Builders: Wartsila Helsinki New Shipyard, Finland

Yard number: 395

Year built: 1972

Original name: *Royal Viking Star*

Lengthened: 1981

Entered service for Fred. Olsen: 15th November 1996

IMO number: 7108930

Length overall (metres): 205.47

Breadth overall (metres): 25.20

Draft (metres): 7.30

Gross tonnage: 28,613

Deadweight tonnage: 5,656

Guests (standard occupancy): 804

Guest cabins: 423

Crew: 320

Speed: 20.0 knots

Machinery: 4 x MAN 7L32/40 diesels

BOUDICCA

Builders: Wartsila Helsinki New Shipyard, Finland

Yard number: 396

Year built: 1973

Original name: *Royal Viking Sky*

Lengthened: 1982

Entered service for Fred. Olsen: 25th February 2006

IMO number: 7218395

Length overall (metres): 205.47

Breadth overall (metres): 25.20

Draft (metres): 7.55

Gross tonnage: 28,388

Deadweight tonnage: 5,956

Guests (standard occupancy): 880

Guest cabins: 463

Crew : 329

Speed: 20.0 knots

Machinery: 4 x MAN 7L32/40 diesels

FotoFlite

Bruce Peter

BALMORAL

Builders: Jos. L Meyer, Papenburg, Germany
Yard number: 616
Year built: 1988
Original name: *Crown Odyssey*
Lengthened: 2008
Entered service for Fred. Olsen: 13th February 2008
IMO number: 8506294
Length overall (metres): 218.18
Breadth overall (metres): 28.20
Draft (metres): 7.25
Gross tonnage: 43,537
Deadweight tonnage: 5,186
Guests (standard occupancy): 1,350
Guest cabins: 710
Crew : 510
Speed: 20.0 knots
Machinery: 4 x MAK 8M601/6M35 diesels 21,300 kW

BRAEMAR

Builders: Union Navale de Levante, Valencia, Spain
Yard number: 198
Year built: 1993
Original name: *Crown Dynasty*
Lengthened: 2008
Entered service for Fred. Olsen: 11th August 2001
IMO number: 9000699
Length overall (metres): 195.92
Breadth overall (metres): 22.50
Draft (metres): 5.40
Gross tonnage: 24,344
Deadweight tonnage: 1,800
Guests (standard occupancy): 929
Guest cabins: 484
Crew : 371
Speed: 17.0 knots
Machinery: 4 x Wartsila 8R22 diesels

Black Watch (John Hendy)

*Top: The figurehead from the 1947 ship **Baldrian** now adorns the aft decks of the **Boudicca**. (John Hendy)*

ACKNOWLEDGEMENTS

My grateful thanks to everyone who has assisted with the compilation of this book, especially to Nathan Philpot, Rachael Jackson and Wendy Jeffreys of the Fred. Olsen Cruise Lines' Public Relations Department in Ipswich who have assisted throughout with promptness and enthusiasm.

Many thanks are also indebted to all those who have kindly offered photographic images for inclusion: Matt Davies, Bruce Peter, John Mavin, Bill Mayes, John May, Andrew Cooke, Marko Stampehl, Richard Seville and FotoFlite. Caroline Hallworth is also thanked for her valuable help in proof reading the finished manuscript.

Thanks also go to my colleague Miles Cowsill for his work involved in the book's design and layout.

BIBLIOGRAPHY

The Fred. Olsen Line and its passenger ships – Anthony Cooke *(Carmania Press – 2007)* Cruise Ships – William Mayes *(Overview Press – 2009)* Complete Guide to Cruising & Cruise Ships 2010 – Douglas Ward *(Berlitz 2009)* Ferry & Cruise Annual 2011 – *(Ferry Publications 2010)* Mediterranean Ferries – Richard Seville *(Ferry Publications 2008)* Ferry & Cruise Review *(Ferry Publications)* Liners & Cruise Ships – Anthony Cooke *(Carmania Press – 1996)* Linjen – the Fred. Olsen Group house magazine Company brochures Material published by FOCL's Public Relations Department.

WEBSITE

Main site: www.fredolsencruises.com